C1

Pebble®

Great African-Americans

Mae
JEMISON

by Luke Colins   Consulting Editor: Gail Saunders-Smith, PhD

CAPSTONE PRESS
a capstone imprint

Pebble Books are published by Capstone Press,
1710 Roe Crest Drive, North Mankato, Minnesota 56003
www.capstonepub.com

Library of Congress Cataloging-in-Publication Data
Colins, Luke.
  Mae Jemison / by Luke Colins.
     pages cm — (Pebble books. Great African-Americans)
  Includes bibliographical references and index.
  Audience: Age 5-7.
  Audience: Grades K to 3.
  Summary: "Simple text and photographs present the life of Mae Jemison"– Provided by publisher.
  ISBN 978-1-4765-3954-6 (library binding)
  ISBN 978-1-4765-5158-6 (paperback)
  ISBN 978-1-4765-6015-1 (ebook pdf)
  1. Jemison, Mae, 1956–Juvenile literature. 2. African American women astronauts—Biography—
Juvenile literature. 3. Astronauts–United States–Biography–Juvenile literature. 4. African
American women scientists–Biography–Juvenile literature. I. Title.
  TL789.85.J46C65 2014
  629.450092—dc23
  [B]   2013037674

Editorial Credits
Anna Butzer, editor; Ashlee Suker, designer; Wanda Winch, media researcher;
Laura Manthe, production specialist

Photo Credits
AP Images: Jim Cooper, 18; Chicago Historical Society, 6; Corbis: Bettmann, 12, NASA/Roger
Ressmeyer, 16; Getty Images/Archive Photos/Harvey Meston, 8; NASA, cover, 4, 10, 14;
Sharppix: Paul Sharp, 20; Shutterstock: buradaki, space design art

Note to Parents and Teachers

The Great African-Americans set supports national curriculum standards for
social studies related to people, places, and environments. This book describes and
illustrates Mae Jemison. The images support early readers in understanding the
text. The repetition of words and phrases helps early readers learn new words. This
book also introduces early readers to subject-specific vocabulary words, which are
defined in the Glossary section. Early readers may need assistance to read some
words and to use the Table of Contents, Glossary, Read More, Internet Sites, and
Index sections of the book.

Printed in the United States of America in North Mankato, Minnesota.
092013   007764CGS14

Table of Contents

Meet Mae

Mae Jemison was the first African-American woman to travel into space. Mae is known for more than being an astronaut. She is also a doctor and teacher.

a science classroom at Mae's high school in Chicago

1956

born in Alabama

6

Young Mae

Mae was born October 17, 1956, in Alabama. At age 3 Mae and her family moved to Chicago. Mae's father was a carpenter. Her mother was a teacher. Mae enjoyed reading and learning about science. She liked learning about outer space.

Cornell University

1956
born in
Alabama

1977
goes to medical
school

After high school Mae went
to Stanford University. She graduated
in 1977 and went to Cornell University.
She studied medicine. Mae graduated
from medical school in 1981.

Astronaut Sally Ride *onboard the* Challenger *space shuttle*

1956
born in
Alabama

1977
goes to medical
school

1983
travels to
Africa

In 1983 Mae joined the Peace Corps. She traveled to Africa and worked as a doctor. That year Sally Ride became the first U.S. woman to go into space. Mae dreamed of being an astronaut too.

1956	1977	1983	1987
born in Alabama	goes to medical school	travels to Africa	becomes astronaut at NASA

As an Adult

Mae returned to the United States.
She applied to NASA to be
an astronaut. She was not chosen
at first. In October 1986 Mae
tried again. In 1987 Mae was
picked by NASA. She began
training to go into space.

The Endeavor *lifts off into space.*

1956
born in
Alabama

1977
goes to medical
school

1983
travels to
Africa

1987
becomes
astronaut at
NASA

14

On September 12, 1992, Mae traveled into space on the shuttle *Endeavor.* She became the first African-American woman to fly on a space mission.

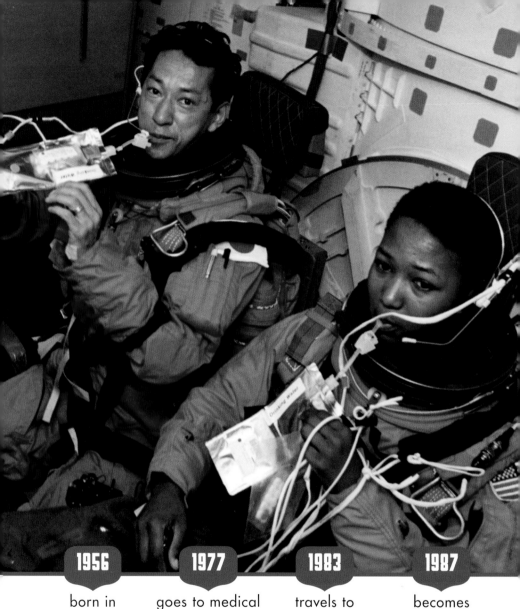

1956	1977	1983	1987
born in Alabama	goes to medical school	travels to Africa	becomes astronaut at NASA

The *Endeavor* spent eight days in space. Mae did science experiments on herself and the crew. She wanted to see what space did to their health. Mae was famous when she returned to Earth.

| 1956 | 1977 | 1983 | 1987 |
| born in Alabama | goes to medical school | travels to Africa | becomes astronaut at NASA |

Later Years

Mae left the NASA space program in March 1993. That year she started the Jemison Group. This company helps poor countries use new medical equipment. In 1994 Mae began a science camp for kids.

1992
flies on
shuttle
Endeavour

1993
leaves NASA;
starts own
company

1994
starts
science camp

1956	1977	1983	1987
born in Alabama	goes to medical school	travels to Africa	becomes astronaut at NASA

Mae continues to help improve medical care in Africa. She is also a professor at Dartmouth's School of Medicine. Mae has worked hard to follow her dreams. Now she is helping others follow theirs.

1992
flies on shuttle *Endeavour*

1993
leaves NASA; starts own company

1994
starts science camp

Glossary

astronaut—a person who is trained to live and work in space

crew—a team of people who work together

experiment—a scientific test to see the effect of something

graduate—to finish all the required classes at a school

NASA—a U.S. government agency that does research on flight and space exploration; NASA stands for National Aeronautics and Space Administration

Peace Corps—an organization of trained volunteers from the United States that helps people in other countries

professor—a teacher with the highest teaching position at a college

Read More

Bennet, Doraine. *Mae Jemison*. Little World Biographies. Vero Beach, Florida: Rourke Pub., 2012.

Braun, Eric. *If I Were an Astronaut*. Dream Big! Minneapolis: Picture Window Books, 2010.

Wheeler, Jill C. *Mae Jemison: Awesome Astronaut*. Women in Science. Minneapolis: ABDO Pub., 2013.

Internet Sites

FactHound offers a safe, fun way to find Internet sites related to this book. All of the sites on FactHound have been researched by our staff.

Here's all you do:
Visit *www.facthound.com*
Type in this code: 9781476539546

Super-cool stuff! Check out projects, games and lots more at **www.capstonekids.com**

Critical Thinking Using the Common Core

1. Mae studied medicine and was a doctor before she became an astronaut. What happened to help Mae realize she wanted to travel into space? (Key Ideas and Details)

2. What has Mae done to help others follow their dreams? Why do you think she wants to help them? (Integration of Knowledge and Ideas)

Index

Word Count: 297
Grade: 1
Early-Intervention Level: 20